# ENGINEERING POWER!

# MACHINES
## IN THE SKY

**Kay Barnham**

Gareth Stevens
PUBLISHING

**Please visit our website, www.garethstevens.com. For a free color catalog of all our high-quality books, call toll free 1-800-542-2595 or fax 1-877-542-2596.**

Cataloging-in-Publication Data

Names: Barnham, Kay.
Title: Machines in the sky / Kay Barnham.
Description:  New York : Gareth Stevens Publishing, 2023. | Series: Engineering power!  | Includes glossary and index.
Identifiers: ISBN 9781538277614 (pbk.) | ISBN 9781538277638 (library bound) | ISBN 9781538277621 (6pack) | ISBN 9781538277645 (ebook)
Subjects: LCSH: Flying machines--Juvenile literature. | Airplanes--Juvenile literature.
Classification: LCC TL547.B376 2023 | DDC 629.13--dc23

Published in 2023 by
**Gareth Stevens Publishing**
29 E. 21st Street
New York, NY 10010

Editor: Elise Short
Design and illustration: Collaborate
Consultant: Andrew Woodward BEng (Hons) CEng MICE FCIArb

**Picture Credits**
Alamy: Avpics 27b; Keystone Press 29b; Stocktrek Images 21b; Zuma Press 14t.
Dreamstime: Michael Klenetsky: 10b.
Shutterstock: Dimitry Birin 28t; Erlo Brown 24b; Anatoli Davydenko 17t; Sergey Denisenko 8t; Angel DiBilio 13b; Everett Historical 10t,17b; FooTToo 9t; Gila Photograpraphy19b; Andrew Harker 15t; IanC66 9b; Ryan Mulhall 28b; Nadezda Murmakova 23c; Bob Pool 21t; Rob1037 25b; Keith Tarrier 29t.
CC Wikimedia Commons: MoorwaySouth 7b.

Printed in the United States of America

CPSIA compliance information: Batch #CSGS23: For further information contact Gareth Stevens, New York, New York at 1-800-542-2595.

Find us on

# Contents

# WHAT DO ENGINEERS DO?

Engineers use science, technology and math to find ways of doing countless different things. So whether it's whizzing around the world, diving beneath the waves, tunneling under the seabed or zooming to the Moon, it's engineers who make that happen.

## MACHINES IN THE SKY

Engineers often design and build a machine to do a certain job. Aircraft for example, are machines that are invented by engineers, so people can fly. But before engineers can even begin to design a flying machine, they have to decide what they want that machine to do. Does it need to fly quickly? Does it need to carry a heavy load? Should there be room for hundreds of passengers or just one? Once they have the answers to these questions—and many more—they can start work!

*The hold is bigger than usual, so there's room for more luggage.*

*Improved air-conditioning, bigger seats and the largest windows on any commercial aircraft mean it's a much more comfortable journey for passengers. New materials used in the cabin mean that there are fewer squeaks too!*

# BOEING 787 DREAMLINER

Engineers didn't just design the Dreamliner (below), which carried its first passengers in 2011, to fly. They designed it to be faster, cheaper to run, quieter, bigger and much more comfortable than earlier passenger jets. And because it was designed to use less fuel, and so releases less carbon-dioxide, the Dreamliner is more environmentally friendly too.

*Half of the fuselage is built from carbon-fiber reinforced plastic, so the Dreamliner is lighter and stronger than other aluminium-body aircraft.*

*Because this is a lighter aircraft, it uses less fuel and is cheaper to run. But as it can carry a lot of fuel, it can also fly a very long way.*

*The wing shape gives the aircraft more lift to carry fuel, cargo and passengers. But it is also designed to be very streamlined, to reduce drag and save fuel.*

*The engines are designed to be efficient—they provide a lot of power for their size. They are quieter than other aircraft engines too.*

*Turn the page to find out all about other fabulous flying machines that engineering power has made possible ...*

# HOT-AIR BALLOONS

When the Montgolfier brothers' hot-air balloon flew up, up and away in 1783, it made history. The balloon became the very first flying machine ever to lift a person into the air and to take them on a—very short—journey.

Inside the burner, liquid propane gas is mixed with air. This fuel is lit to produce a flame, which heats the air in the balloon.

The balloon's envelope is made of strong, light nylon.

The pilot and passengers travel inside a gondola.

The Montgolfier brothers' hot-air balloons were made from silk, paper and taffeta. Now, they are made from nylon.

## GOING UP ... AND DOWN

The science behind hot-air balloons is simple. Hot air is lighter than cool air. So when the air inside a balloon is heated by a burner, the air rises—taking the balloon with it. When the air cools, it falls and is reheated, rising again to keep the balloon in the air. When the burner is switched off, the air cools and the balloon sinks.

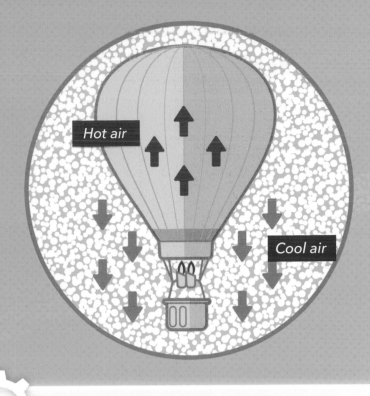

Hot air

Cool air

## WHERE THE WIND BLOWS

Hot-air balloons don't have steering wheels. But because the wind blows in different directions at different altitudes, pilots can use these air currents to take balloons where they want to go. All they have to do is make the balloon go up or down, so that it is blown along by different air currents that change its direction.

## EXTREME ENGINEERING!

In 1987, the *Virgin Atlantic Flyer* became the first hot-air balloon to cross the Atlantic. Its envelope was as big as a tower block. The lower half of the balloon's envelope was made of a fabric that absorbed the Sun's energy and heated the air inside. This meant that the burners needed to use less propane gas to lift the balloon.

*The Virgin Atlantic Flyer's capsule was pressurized so that it could fly at high altitudes. It was surrounded by propane tanks that could be dropped to save weight when they were empty.*

# AIRSHIPS

Airships fly because they are filled with gas that is lighter than air. But unlike hot-air balloons, these flying machines are powered by engines. They can also be steered. The first powered airship was built in 1852 by French engineer, Henri Giffard.

*Early airships like this Zeppelin were filled with hydrogen gas. But because hydrogen caught fire very easily, all modern airships use helium instead.*

Envelope

Gondola

Engine

## SAILING THROUGH THE SKIES

Airships got their name because they looked like they floated in the air. They are actually filled with helium gas, which makes them float. Air (which is heavier than helium) can be pumped into the balloon to make it go lower, and released to make it rise. Engines propel them forwards and stabilizers change their direction and height.

# SPOT THE DIFFERENCE!

Dirigibles and blimps are both types of airship, but it's easy to tell them apart. A dirigible is a rigid airship: it has a stiff metal frame inside the envelope. It can be identified by the ridges that run along its sides. But a blimp has no framework. It keeps its shape because it's filled with helium gas, like a party balloon. Its sides are smooth. Blimps are often used for advertising ... in the sky!

Vertical stabilizer

Horizontal stabilizer

# EXTREME ENGINEERING!

The *Airlander 10* is a hybrid airship that is part-airship, part-airplane and part-helicopter. Its body acts like a huge wing to create lift. Its four powerful diesel engines allow it to travel at speeds of up to 92 miles per hour (148 kph).

*In 2018, the Airlander 10 was the world's longest aircraft.*

# AIRPLANES

In 1903, something fabulous happened: Wilbur and Orville Wright designed and built an airplane that flew! The *Wright Flyer* didn't use hot air or gas. The pioneering flying machine had a piston engine, a propeller and wings.

*The* Wright Flyer *was made from wood, fabric and wire. It succeeded because its engine was light and powerful enough to get the aircraft off the ground. On its first flight, the* Wright Flyer *flew almost 853 feet (260 m)!*

## EXTREME ENGINEERING!

The Hughes H-4 Hercules was the largest wooden aircraft ever built. It was nicknamed the *Spruce Goose*, even though it was mostly made of birch and not spruce trees. But despite having eight engines, it was still too heavy to fly properly. Improvements in engine technology and lighter materials have now made it possible for larger planes to fly.

*Each of the Spruce Goose's propellers measured over 16.4 feet (5 m) wide.*

## UP, UP AND AWAY!

An airplane needs to go both forwards and up to take off. Smaller aircraft usually have a piston engine, in which pistons move up and down inside cylinders to create power. The engine turns the propeller. And as it spins, the propeller pulls the airplane along the runway. When the airplane accelerates, air flows quickly over its wings.

## THE SECRET OF THE WINGS

The shape of an airplane's wings is very important. Because the top of a wing is curved, air molecules are directed over the wing and then downwards. Air molecules that collide with the flatter underside of a wing are squashed, so air pressure is increased. Less air pressure above the wing and more air pressure below creates lift, which makes the airplane go up!

*Flaps extend to make the wings bigger, so that the aircraft can fly slower to make landing easier.*

*Because the wings are higher than the cockpit, it's easier to see the runway when landing.*

*Ailerons are used to bank left and right.*

Wing

Fuel tank

*The horizontal stabilizer is used to pitch the nose up and down.*

Rudder

*The vertical stabilizer turns the aircraft's nose left and right.*

Engine

Propeller

Fuselage

Landing gear

*The Cessna 172 (above) might be small, but it's sturdy, reliable and easy to fly. Since 1955, well over 40,000 have been produced, making it the most successful airplane design ever.*

# JET AIRCRAFT

The invention of the jet engine in 1930 changed air travel forever. Jet engines are more powerful, more reliable and easier to fix than piston engines, because they have fewer moving parts. They can also fly at much higher altitudes, where they use less fuel and are more efficient. The air there is thinner, so they can fly faster too!

*Flap*

*The A380's two decks split the aircraft into three compartments-two decks for passengers and one for cargo.*

*Wings*

*Viewed from the front, the body of an A380 is not circular or even oval. It's shaped like a figure 8. This is where it gets its name from.*

*Fuselage*

*In an emergency, the A380 can fly with just one engine running.*

## JET POWER!

In the high-bypass jet engine, most of the air travels around the engine. This reduces noise and provides most of the thrust. The remaining air is then squeezed through a compressor and fuel is added. When the mixture of air and fuel is lit, it shoots out of the back of the engine as a jet of hot gas. And because this fiery jet pushes backwards, the airplane is pushed forwards through the air.

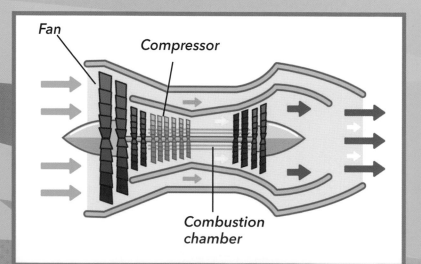

*Fan*

*Compressor*

*Combustion chamber*

Fuel

Winglet

## THE AMAZING A380

Passenger jets are usually powered by two, three or four jet engines, depending on their size. The Airbus A380 (left) has four jet engines and is the world's largest passenger airliner yet. A triple-decker with a wide body and four engines, it can carry as many as 853 passengers and fly up to 932 miles (15,000 km) without refueling!

## EXTREME ENGINEERING!

The Gulfstream G650ER's two Rolls-Royce jet engines mean that this business jet can fly at speeds of up to 690 mph (1,111 kph). It can also travel for 8,631 miles (13,890 km) without refueling. Up to 19 passengers can whizz from Hong Kong to New York City in one trip!

*The G650ER is not designed for cheap travel. It is designed to speed passengers to their destination in comfort.*

13

# SUPERSONIC AIRCRAFT

A supersonic airplane can fly faster than sound, which travels through air at 761 mph (1,225 kph). The speed of sound has its own name —Mach 1. Any object that can travel at more than five times the speed of sound —or Mach 5—is officially hypersonic.

*SpaceShipOne and SpaceShipTwo are spaceplanes that have reached hypersonic speeds.*

*Engines contain intake ramps to help slow down the incoming air. This allows the engines to work efficiently at supersonic speed.*

*The mini undercarriage under the tail stops it hitting the ground during take-off and landing.*

*The undercarriage is taller than usual because the aircraft takes off and lands at a much steeper angle than usual.*

## FLY LIKE THE WIND

Supersonic aircraft are mostly used for defense or research. But two passenger aircraft were designed, built and operated in the 1960s. Both flew very high and very fast. The Soviet Tu-144 cruised at 52,493 feet (16,000 m) at Mach 1.6. Meanwhile, the British and French Concorde (see right) could fly at an altitude of 60,039.4 feet (18,300 m) at Mach 2.02. It set a world record for a passenger jet when it flew from New York City to London in just 2 hours, 52 minutes and 59 seconds as opposed to 6 hours and 50 minutes on a regular passenger jet. It was retired in 2003.

# EXTREME ENGINEERING!

The Eurofighter Typhoon is an astonishingly fast fighter jet. It's powered by two Eurojet EJ200 turbofan engines, which can power the aircraft along at speeds of up to Mach 2—or twice the speed of sound. This is nearly two and a half times times faster than an A380 (see pages 12–13).

*Elevons on the wing are a combination of elevators and ailerons.*

*Delta-shaped wing.*

*The Eurofighter can perform such topsy-turvy moves that pilots sometimes get dizzy. If this happens, they simply press a button in the cockpit and the aircraft turns itself the right way up again, flying slowly until the pilot feels better.*

*Concorde could reach an altitude of over 59,055 feet (18,000 m). From that height, passengers could see the curvature of Earth from its windows.*

*The nose droops to allow the pilot to see the runway.*

# GLIDERS

Some aircraft don't need an engine to fly. A glider has no engine at all! Gliders do need the help of another aircraft to take off, but once they are in the sky, they can stay there for hours.

## POWERLESS FLIGHT

Because they have no engine to power them, gliders are designed to use as little energy as possible. They are very small—there is just enough room for one or two people inside the cockpit. They are also made from lightweight materials such as fiberglass and carbon-fiber. Meanwhile, their wings are long (to give them as much lift as possible) and narrow (to reduce drag).

## FLY LIKE A BIRD

A powered aircraft pulls a glider into the air using a tow rope. Sometimes, a winch can be used from the ground. Then the glider is on its own, free to soar through the air like a bird, using thermals—columns of rising warm air —to fly higher again and again.

*There are small skids or castors on the tips of the wings or under the tail too.*

*Canopy*

*Air brakes are used to increase drag and slow the glider down.*

*Flap*

*The main wheel supports most of the weight of the glider on landing.*

*Gliders are smooth and streamlined, so they glide through the air as easily as possible.*

*Aileron*

Make your own glider! That's
exactly what a paper airplane is.

*Cockpit*

# EXTREME ENGINEERING!

In 1981,the Space Shuttle used its three main engines and two rocket boosters
for lift-off. When it returned to Earth, it flew in the same way as a glider,
although a much heavier one. The spacecraft was designed to slow from
7,301 miles per hour (11,750 kph) in orbit to 248.5 miles per hour (400 kph) by
the time it touched down.

*The Space Shuttle was a reusable spacecraft that took off
like a rocket and landed like an unpowered glider.*

# HELICOPTERS

A helicopter is capable of vertical take-off and landing (VTOL). It can fly forwards, backwards and sideways. It can turn in almost any direction. It can even hover in one place. A helicopter can do so much more than an airplane because, instead of fixed wings, it has a rotor.

Tail rotor

Engine

Main rotor

Blade

Fuselage

Cockpit

Landing skid

## SPINNING AROUND AND AROUND

A helicopter's rotor is a group of two or more rotor blades that are connected to the aircraft's engine. Rotor blades are shaped like mini aircraft wings. So when they spin round, they create lift to pull the helicopter into the air. When the blades are tilted, the helicopter changes direction.

*A helicopter doesn't need a runway, so it can access out-of-reach places that an aircraft can't. Most helicopters have a tail rotor, which spins vertically. This stops the main rotor from spinning the helicopter's fuselage around and around. It also helps to steer.*

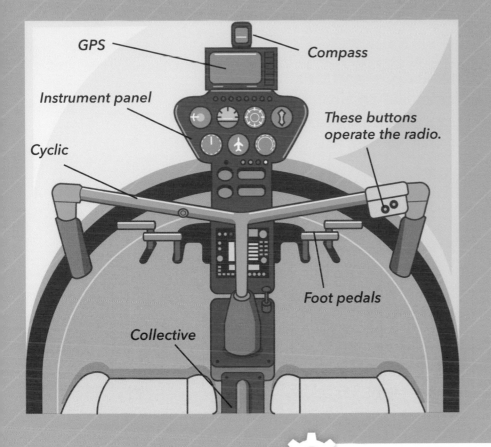

GPS

Compass

Instrument panel

These buttons operate the radio.

Cyclic

Foot pedals

Collective

Helicopters might be able to perform plenty of tricky maneuvers, but helicopter pilots need to be super skillful to do them. At the same time as holding the cyclic (which controls the direction) with one hand, they hold the collective (which makes the helicopter go up and down, and also controls the engine speed) with the other, while their feet operate the foot pedals (which make the helicopter turn left and right). It's trickier than it looks!

# EXTREME ENGINEERING!

The Erickson S-64 Aircrane has two engines so that it can lift extremely heavy weights. When fitted with a 2,642 gallons (10,000 liters) water tank, this mighty helicopter can be used to control bush fires and forest fires, by dumping load after load of water onto flames.

*It takes just 45 seconds for the Aircrane to refill a water tank. If the tank is removed, the helicopter can be used for heavy lifting.*

19

# TILTROTORS

What do you get if you cross a helicopter and an airplane? A tiltrotor! This hybrid aircraft looks like an airplane, but can take off and land vertically, like a helicopter. Tiltrotors can also take off and land more like an airplane, with a much shorter runway than usual.

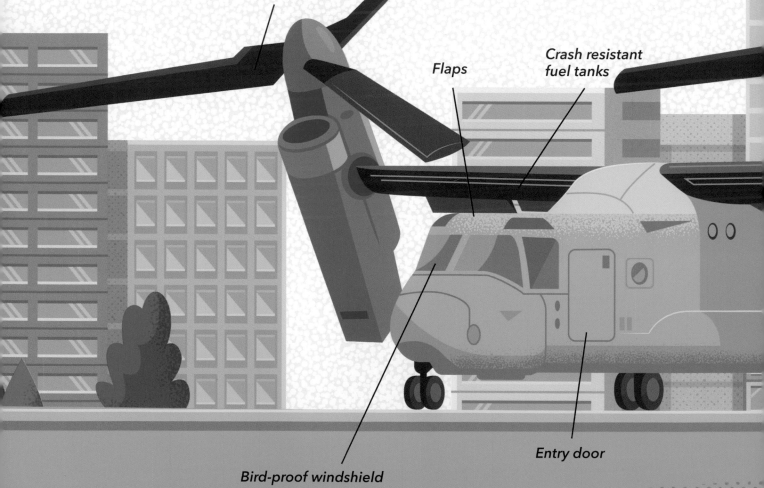

25 feet (7.6 m) diameter rotors

Flaps

Crash resistant fuel tanks

Bird-proof windshield

Entry door

*Tiltrotors can fly faster and further than helicopters, without refueling.*

## HYBRID SUPERSTAR

A tiltrotor has rotors that ... tilt! Its rotors are usually mounted at the end of fixed wings. For vertical take-off, the rotors are tilted upwards so that they face the sky. They then spin horizontally like a helicopter's rotor to lift the aircraft up and into the air. Once the tiltrotor is airborne, the rotors gradually tilt forwards until they are spinning vertically. Now, it looks like an airplane. Acting as propellers, the rotors pull the aircraft through the air.

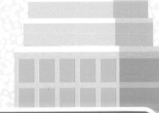

*Pitch change lever*

*Flaperons*

## EXTREME ENGINEERING!

The CV-22 Osprey tiltrotor has LED lights on the tip of each rotor blade. During military maneuvers, these mean the aircraft can be seen at night. It's also easier to spot them when the weather is bad. These tip lights are only visible to those wearing night-vision goggles.

# STEALTH AIRCRAFT

Stealth aircraft are designed to fly through the sky on top-secret missions, without anyone knowing they are there. Normal aircraft can be detected using a system called radar. But stealth aircraft are specially designed to avoid radar and stay totally hidden.

## HOW RADAR WORKS

Radar is an ingenius way of keeping track of aircraft. It works by sending radio waves from an antenna into the sky. When these waves hit an aircraft, they are bounced back to the antenna. The length of time it takes the radio waves to return means it's possible to work out how far away the aircraft is.

## HIDING FROM RADAR

Stealth aircraft mostly fly at night, so it's too dark to see them. (When they're on a mission, they don't use their lights.) But it's also difficult for radar to detect them, because they are flat and pointy, making radio waves ping away in different directions. Meanwhile, some surfaces are designed to absorb radio waves. Either way, the radio waves do not return to the antenna. It's as if the aircraft isn't there ...

*Structures designed to absorb radar*

Wing tip

Outboard elevon

Mid elevon

Inboard elevon

Beaver tail pitch control system

As this aircraft has no tail at all, split rudders are flaps that open up like an air brake, using drag to turn the aircraft like a rudder would.

# EXTREME ENGINEERING!

To prepare for long-range missions, crews spend as long as 48 hours in a flight simulator. But as it's impossible to stay focused for so long, during a mission there are two crews, which take turns flying and sleeping in the area behind the cockpit.

Inside a flight simulator, it's just like a real aircraft! In this passenger airplane flight simulator, pilots train in a safe environment.

# DRONES

Drones are also known as Unmanned Aerial Vehicles—or UAVs for short. They were first used for dangerous military missions. But now drones of different shapes and sizes are used for many different jobs, such as search and rescue, photography and even delivering food and medicine to disaster zones.

*The quadcopter's four propellers mean that it is more stable and easier to fly.*

## DOWN TO EARTH

Like other aircraft, drones do need someone to fly them. But that person isn't on board; they operate the drone by remote control from the ground.

*Drones can carry high-definition cameras or video cameras.*

*Landing gear*

*Some drones are small enough to fit in the palm of your hand! This one even has a camera.*

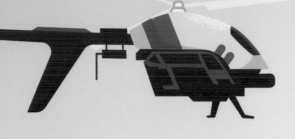

## DIFFERENT DRONES

Fixed-wing drones need a runway to take off and land, just like airplanes. They can fly quickly and carry heavy loads. Rotary drones are much more like helicopters. They have rotors and can take off and land vertically. Quadcopters have four rotors—spinning these at different speeds means it's possible to steer the drone. It can even hover in one place!

— *A tiny motor powers each propeller.*

## EXTREME ENGINEERING!

In New South Wales, Australia, lifeguard drones fly along the shoreline, their onboard video cameras watching out for danger. If a shark is spotted, the drone's megaphone is used to warn swimmers. The drones can also be used to drop inflatable rescue pods into the sea, when swimmers are in distress.

*UAVs are helping to keep Australian beaches safe.*

# JETPACKS

Jetpacks? Rocket belts? Hoverboards? They sound as if they belong to science fiction. But they're actually science fact. These personal aircraft are capable of vertical take-off and landing. They're also a whole lot of fun.

*The hoop is for head protection.*

*The pilot wears the jetpack like a backpack. A set of straps holds it firmly to the body. When the jetpack is running, these straps lift the wearer into the air.*

*The yaw twist grip allows the pilot to turn left or right. The other twist grip gives more power or thrust, either to take off or land or, if you're flying, go faster or slower.*

## ROCKET-POWERED FLIGHT

Personal VTOL aircraft use either miniature rockets or jet engines to provide lift. When these are pointed downwards, the pilot goes up, just like a rocket. Hand-held controls allow the pilot to adjust direction and speed.

Even though personal aircraft were invented over fifty years ago, they're still not very common. They are difficult to fly—even for an expert, it's dangerous. And it takes a lot of fuel to push someone upwards to escape Earth's gravity. The small amount of fuel that a pilot can carry is only enough for a very short flight. But engineers are working hard to build increasingly better flying machines.

engines
k in air and
w jet gases
wnwards.

# EXTREME ENGINEERING!

Richard Browning, from the UK, invented the Jet Suit 3—
a made-to-measure suit with built-in jet engines. These
give enough downwards thrust to push the wearer
upwards to an altitude of over 11,811 feet (3,600 m) and
to travel at speeds of over 31 mph (50 kph). The jet suit
went on sale in 2018. It was very, very expensive: about
$453,866 (£340,000)!

*The Jet Suit 3 is powered by five kerosene-fuelled micro gas
turbines—two on each arm and one on the back.*

# MORE MAGNIFICENT MACHINES

## ANTONOV AN-225 MRIYA

This is the largest and heaviest aircraft in the world, with a wingspan of 290 feet (88.4 m) and six engines. One of its main jobs is to transport the Russian Buran space shuttle to the launch site. Buran is not loaded inside the An-225—it's carried on top, like a roofbox on a car.

*The Antonov An-225 Mriya's landing gear has 32 wheels!*

## SPACESHIPONE

In 2004, *SpaceShipOne* became the first privately owned space plane to achieve suborbital flight. Designed and built by Burt Rutan and his company—Scaled Composites—it was launched in mid-air from underneath its carrier plane, called *White Knight*. Then *SpaceShipOne's* hybrid rocket motors took over, blasting it upwards.

*SpaceShipOne (below) and White Knight (above) took off together before separating at a height of 49,212.6 feet (15,000 m).*

# LOCKHEED SR-71 BLACKBIRD

This is the fastest piloted air-breathing aircraft ever built, so far. The Lockheed SR-71 Blackbird broke the world record in 1976 with a speed of 2,193.2 mph (3,529.6 kph) or Mach 2.88. That's nearly 37.3 miles (60 km) every minute.

*The Lockheed SR-71 Blackbird is made of titanium, to make it strong and light enough to fly at supersonic speeds.*

# THE *FLYING BEDSTEAD*

Its official name was the Rolls-Royce Thrust Measuring Rig. But the metal frame, four legs and castors surrounding the engine made it look more like a bed, which is how it got its nickname. It was hard to believe that the *Flying Bedstead* could fly—but it did. This experimental aircraft pioneered vertical take-off and landing and first flew in 1954.

*The* Flying Bedstead *is now displayed in the Science Museum in London.*

# GLOSSARY

**aileron**
a hinged part of a wing that can be moved to control flight

**altitude**
height above sea level

**carbon fiber**
a strong, light material

**cargo**
goods carried from one place to another

**delta**
a triangle shape

**drag**
the force that acts against the direction of movement

**elevon**
the hinged part of a delta wing that can be moved to control flight

**envelope**
the fabric part of a hot-air balloon that holds the air

**fuselage**
the main body of an aircraft

**hold**
the area where luggage is stored in an aircraft

**hybrid**
something that is a mixture of different things

**lift**
the force on the wing of a bird or aircraft that keeps it in the air as it moves forward

**piston**
a short cylinder that moves up and down inside a tube

**pitch**
the rotation of an airplane from wingtip to wingtip. This movement makes the airplane's nose and tail move up and down. This controls the ascent and descent of the airplane.

**propane**
a flammable gas

**propeller**
a device with two or more blades that spin

**radar**
short for radio detection and ranging, this is a system that shows the location and speed of different objects such as aircraft

**rotor**
a device with two or more blades that spin

**rudder**
a hinged device at the rear of a boat that is used for steering

**streamlined**
designed in a way that makes movement easier through air or water

**suborbital**
a space journey that does not go all the way round a planet

**taffeta**
a type of fabric

**thrust**
the force that pushes a jet or rocket engine forward as it takes off

**tow rope**
a rope or chain that a vehicle uses to pull another vehicle

**winch**
a machine that lifts heavy objects by turning a chain or rope around a tube-shaped device

# WEBSITES

*howthingsfly.si.edu/activities*
Have fun with these educational activities from the Smithsonian National Air and Space Museum.

*kids.kiddle.co/Wright_brothers*
Find out more about the Wright brothers' historic flight.

*kiwico.com/blog/2018/01/26/5-amazing-flying-machines-you-can-make/*
Make your own flying machines!

*grc.nasa.gov/www/k-12/UEET/StudentSite/dynamicsofflight.html*
NASA explains how aircraft fly.

# BOOKS

*100 Facts: Flight*
by Sue Becklake (Miles Kelly Publishing Ltd, 2010)

*DK Eyewitness Books: Flight*
(DK Publishing, 2011)

*Flight School*
by Nick Barnard (Thames and Hudson, 2012)

*It'll Never Work: Planes and Helicopters*
by Jon Richards (Franklin Watts, 2019)

*Planes*
by Fiona Patchett (Usborne, 2007)

*The Tech-Head Guide: Drones*
by William Potter (Wayland, 2020)

# INDEX